The Power Hug

Memoirs of a Mom

Linda L. Still

ISBN 978-1-105-70919-7
Cover Art Drawn by Jason Morris

DEDICATION

This book is dedicated to the three children who have taught me about unconditional love. To Jonathan, Andrew and Jennifer – thank you for letting me love you so much and for teaching me that each of us is an individual and special in our own right. You are the joys in my life and never does a moment pass that you are not in my heart and soul. To Meredith and Jason, my "daughter" and "son," I could not have picked better additions to our family. And to my husband, Tom (Dolly), my partner for the past 38 years, through all the ups and downs of child-rearing – a wonderful Dad to our children and always supportive of me – thank you for your love. To Uncle Mike for always being there; and Nicholas, my wonderful Godson, for making me so proud of you. To Sitto and Gege – thank you for providing our children with a "village" and the most special love ever.

XOXOXO

MY MANTRA

Never let an opportunity pass to speak with, listen to or see my children, even if it's only for a second. The opportunity may not present itself again and I don't want to miss the gift I get each time I see them or hear their voices.

FORWARD

For as long as I can remember, I have wanted to write a book about children. Although there are many how-to books available, I see this as different. As a speech and language pathologist for the public school system for the past 34 years, I have come in contact with many parents who are truly seeking parenting skills. Most of them are doing many of the things I would recommend both as a language professional and as a parent. However, they do not always recognize the importance of all the little things they do. I hope this book will bring a few chuckles and some "ah-hah" moments; recognition of some of the things you have seen in your own families and an awareness to those who read it about how important it is to communicate with children on all levels and how much fun it can be to raise children if one is willing to put in the time and effort. Parenting is a somewhat thankless job in that your child does not go to bed each evening saying "thanks for timing me out today" or even "thanks for dinner!" It isn't until years later, perhaps when they are in college or have their own children, that they can truly appreciate the sacrifices made for them. Nevertheless, it is our responsibility as parents to provide our children with opportunities and expose them to various arenas, in order that they will someday be responsible adults able to take care of themselves and their own children.

Some may be asking what qualifies me to author this book. Who knows! I am the mother of three grown children. Jonathan, 33, is a practicing psychiatrist. An easy child to raise, he set the tone for our family in terms of study habits and overall disposition. His mild demeanor and enthusiasm for learning made him a teacher's dream! Very goal-oriented, Jonathan was quite successful in school and always a bit more mature than others his age. He always sets his eyes on the prize and would work as hard as he needed to in order to obtain it. He was the quintessential first-born and continues to have the same loving spirit he did as a little boy. Andrew, 31, is a lawyer, passing the California BAR exam on his first try! He is very different from his brother in many ways, yet just as focused and goal oriented! I cannot tell you how many times in the last 31 years I have wondered how two boys born only 18 months apart could be so different! Andrew has probably taught me the most about accepting people for who they are and that wondrous word, "compromise!" I have learned to look at each person as an individual with special qualities particular to them. His kind heart and gentle soul show me constantly that he is wise beyond his years. Jennifer, 29, graduated from college in three and a half years and works as a dentist in Southern California. She is a wonderful mix of her brothers and my "right hand girl." I can depend on her for anything and she seems to know my needs before I have them! When I look into her eyes I see an "updated" version of myself! Also, I have been a speech and language pathologist for two different school districts in California since 1977. I have worked all grade levels, from preschool through high school. I currently am the speech pathologist for an elementary school district as a member of the assessment team that looks at approximately 150 preschoolers each year, ranging from articulation disorders to autism, medically fragile, and everything in between. I also work as a speech therapist in a private clinic, primarily with children with autism. I am sure that I continue to enjoy my job because it gives me an opportunity to "mother!" Being a mom is the job I love the best, and it is what I am before anything else. Watching your children grow into happy, healthy and productive adults is the greatest gift of all.

GIFTS FROM GOD

When I was seven months pregnant with Jonathan, my first child, my father had a stroke and passed away. I remember thinking over and over again how God can take one person and put another in his place on this earth. This was definitely the case for our family. We wallowed away the days of our grief by looking forward to this new life which was forthcoming. It is incredible how much happiness one feels when they are anticipating the birth of a child, even when their hearts are filled with so much sadness.

For months my husband and I had talked about what to name our new baby. We always knew what the boy's name would be, but the girl's name had yet to be decided. With the death of my father, we knew that if this baby were a boy, he would be Jonathan George, named after my dad, but also meaning "a gift from God." It was at the precise moment of his birth that I realized that children are precious "gifts," and as parents we are given a rare opportunity to be part of molding a human being through the various stages of life.

In order to fully appreciate the wonders of parenthood, people have to look beyond and sometimes even forget the day to day attention that children need. Parenting is an incredible job, which nobody prepares you for. There are no practical manuals, and even though there are many books and classes, it would be impossible to predict what each parent might encounter from day-to-day with each individual child and their particular personality. Kids are a full time job! It's not until you tuck them into bed at night and see this peaceful, beautiful little person, that one can appreciate the beauty of this gift.

With all of our children being so different from each other, sometimes the best way I found for handling all the issues that arose was to step back and remember that these children were only given to me for a short period of time. As the days, months and years flew by, their lives became busier and I had less time with them. Although they needed me less in some ways, they needed me more in others. And sometimes the chaos was too much to stand! It was at these times that I would try to remember that this would not be forever, and that someday I would feel sad and somewhat lonely when the commotion was gone. Children are a gift – although they are with us forever in that they will always be our children, we only have a hand in their lives for a relatively short amount of time. To spend much of this time thinking about how exhausting it is to raise kids and how unappreciative they are is a waste of time and energy! Instead, seize each moment that you can and try to enjoy as many of them as you can. So many "firsts" happen in a child's life, but they are only "first" once. From the first smile to the first step, the first word spoken to the first word read, the first soccer game to the first big dance, the first day of kindergarten to the first day of college - they are all firsts, each as special as the one before it, and different for every child. Love and enjoy each of these with your child, because you truly cannot go back.

TRADITIONS

I believe that traditions are one of the greatest gifts we can give our children. Traditions instill a sense of security and bonding in all people, but particularly children who, no matter how old, look forward to the rituals and all the "pomp and circumstance" that comes with certain times of their lives. These traditions can be for anything deemed worthy of being remembered time after time. They do not need to be associated with major holidays or events, but can be as simple as ice cream sundaes to celebrate the completion of a report card period. Positive reinforcement can be built into many activities and accomplishments throughout a child's lifetime and all kids deserve to be recognized for their successes. It is totally unfair to expect any two children to perform the exact same way, and even their methods for achieving their goals may vary. Accept your child for who he is and do everything in your power not to compare him or her to his siblings or another child. Loss of self-confidence is probably one of the greatest detriments that a child places on himself. Once he does not believe in himself or thinks that you do not believe in him, he will stop trying. Perish the thought!

Anyway, back to traditions. I like to turn anything I can into a tradition. Some of them are more obvious, such as letting each child pick whatever he wants Mom or Dad to cook for him on his birthday. Trust me, there have been times when I would be cursing while preparing a complete Chinese dinner that I could have gotten from the local take-out restaurant for half the cost and fuss! But it would not be the same as the fun Andrew had going through the cookbook and picking out everything from soup to dessert. And whenever I complained about cooking something messy, he was the first to remind me that he could pick Chinese again for this birthday dinner and I would have to do it all over again! It was a private joke and better yet ... a connection. Besides, he knew whatever he wanted me to prepare, I would. Afterall, it's tradition!

Something else that we started when the kids were little began when Jonathan was about 6-½ years of age. One day, this inquisitive kindergartner informed me that he did not feel that he had enough time with his dad and me alone. Having three children in 3-½ years made things tight for alone time! My husband and I came up with a plan that we initiated with all three children, even Jennifer who at that time was about three. Each month, it was one child's turn to pick a restaurant of their choice for dinner out with Mom and Dad. We set stipulations, however. The restaurant could not be fast food and the child who was dining out had to wear "Sunday" clothes. When we first started, because the children were still fairly young, we frequented nicer coffee shop type establishments. The boys were capable of picking their own restaurants, but we helped Jennifer with her decisions for a couple of years. We would get a baby-sitter for the children staying home and that was a night that my husband would get home from work early enough so we would not have to have a late dinner. The conversation was centered around our "dinner guest," who was always excited to have so much attention. This tradition continued to the high school years and the kinds of restaurants certainly changed! As it turned out for our family, each child ended up with his birthday month as his month for dinner. They each had four opportunities a year for quality time with Mom and Dad. I had many friends tell me that it worked for us because we had more than two children, and that they didn't think they could do it if they had to leave one at home. I can understand what they are saying, but with the right baby-sitter and perhaps a special dinner treat, as well as the expectation that next month is their turn, I think this can be fun for any family. It provided us with a lot of special times with each of our children and the opportunity for them to have something they really looked forward to. Perhaps this was the beginning of our “foodies!”

Some of our other traditions have included the ceremonial ornament-of-the-year! Each year since they were born, each child received an ornament that represented something special that had occurred in their life during that year. For instance, when Jonathan studied penguins in first grade and became a "Penguin

Pro," he received a penguin ornament to represent that year for him. Andrew adored popcorn, and got a popcorn popper ornament one year. Other times, the ornaments were significant because of a family vacation to Hawaii or Mexico, a school desk for the beginning of school, a piano for the year they began lessons and of course the "car ornament" for their 16th year. The theory behind this was that as the children would have their own homes and families, they would at least start their first few Christmas' with some special ornaments that would hopefully bring back meaningful memories. And the pomp and circumstance that went along with receiving the ornament was half the fun (for my husband and I, that is)! The new ornaments were always given after the lights had been put on the tree, but before any other ornaments were hung. Everyone knew and looked forward to the routine. As they went off to college and would not get home until just days prior to Christmas, we would save the giving of the ornaments until the night they come home. The older they got, the "cheesier" were the pictures - after all, now they were "humoring" us!

Associated with Christmas was our annual "fancy" holiday dinner. When the children were younger, I would prepare a nice dinner that we would eat in the dining room, set of course with china and crystal. Everyone had to dress-up - it's amazing how behaviors change when you eat in the dining room! As the kids got older, we began making reservations for a nice dinner out on the weekend before Christmas. We always chose a restaurant that we would not normally go to, making it even more special. At least a month before Christmas, we would start looking at which restaurant we wanted to go to! I guess we truly bred kids who love to eat!! Another thing that we looked forward to was our annual New Year's fondue. Before Tom and I had children, alone or with special friends, we would celebrate New Year's Eve/Day with fondue. Accompanied by a great salad and lots of bread, we would leisurely sit and spend what seemed like hours talking and eating. As our children got older, we often would stay home on New Year's Eve and they began eating fondue with us. Even as they've gotten older and have lives of their own, we still try to incorporate fondue into the holidays – after all, it's tradition!

Traditions truly can be anything you want them to be. Consistency is the key. I liked to bake bread and on Valentine's Day I would put red food coloring in the water so we could have pink bread. For St. Patrick's Day (Andrew's Birthday), I did the same thing with green food coloring. I sliced the bread for their sandwiches and toast in the morning. The other children at school came to look forward to the various-colored bread. Do anything you like and that your children look forward to. Sometimes, as the years go on, it seems that no one really cares anymore. But they do, and if you don't do what they have come to expect, then you realize how they miss it. Before they left for college, I wondered what I would do about some of our traditions. But I found out. I couldn't bear the thought of finals week without a "goody box" of their favorite things to nibble and a note reminding them how much I believed in them.

Also wonderful to receive are unexpected and expected notes. Nothing is more fun for a child than to open his lunch bag and find a message written on a napkin or a happy face note with kisses and hugs (xoxoxo) all over it. When these traditions are started young, it's amazing how accepting children are of these as they get older. Sometimes the sentiment has to be a bit more discreet, but everyone knows how to interpret it. Also, I found that notes could be a very effective way to communicate to children things you wanted them to do. For instance, I have always been a working Mom. There were times in their lives when I would have to go to work before them or on a day that they had no school. If they were home alone, as they were when they were older, I would leave a note at each of their places at the kitchen table with a list of things I would like them to accomplish before I got home that day. Some of the items on the list included things such as homework and chores, while a few things were fun such as "watch Price is Right at 10:00!" Similarly, when someone was staying with them when they were younger, I would include things on the list such as playing their favorite game or talking to their best friend.

Once again, I am always flabbergasted when I don't do something and someone reminds me that I forgot! It's was always tradition in our family that the children would, from time to time, come home from school and find a love note and their favorite candy awaiting them on their pillow (especially sour cherries)! When each of the boys went away to college, of course this could not continue in the same way, but whenever they would come home for a weekend visit or at their breaks, they would find a love note and candy on their pillow welcoming them home. I can't forget the time that Andrew came home for summer, and I forgot to have the note and candy waiting for him. As soon as he got home and took his things upstairs to his room, I heard this whining voice yelling, "Where's my note and my candy!" I couldn't believe it! Even at his age, the consistency of something that reminded him of love and familiarity was important, even when it was from Mom!

Another tradition that we started so many years ago was the annual "Oscar Night Hors' D'ouevres" Party! I am a confirmed star struck nut! Watching the Academy Awards would not be the same if we didn't set a buffet table with various appetizers and turn the television on at 3:00 in the afternoon. We would serve sparkling cider in champagne flutes when the children were younger and graduated to margaritas when "we were all old enough!" The funny part of all this is that even though the kids are rarely home for this television event any more, they always ask if I made some of their favorite appetizers! In today's health conscious age, most of these would not be allowed! Nevertheless, they are still being made and enjoyed by whoever can participate. After all, anything is okay in moderation!!!

Similar to the candy on the pillow, was the Halloween tradition of each child getting a mini-pumpkin. As soon as they were available in the stores in early October, I would buy each of the children a mini-pumpkin for their room. It was accompanied by, yes, a love note! Even when they first went off to college, the pumpkin would arrive by mail with a "goody box" of candy and cookies.

All of these traditions were so easy to institute and did not cost much money. In many instances, they hardly took any extra time! They do, however, validate your child by letting them know their importance. Children who know they are loved and respected will have less chances of suffering from low self-esteem and insecurities.

IT TAKES A VILLAGE

Most people have heard the saying, "It takes a village to raise a child." I truly believe that there is a lot of truth to this statement. In times gone by, families were composed of extended family that lived with or very near each other. Everyone took part in raising children. In every way, from discipline to religion, all those who had contact with the child contributed in some way to their upbringing. As long as the philosophy is the same, a child grows up knowing that many people care about their well-being. Today, many people have chosen where they live based on economics. Jobs often dictate where we live and often it has little, if any, proximity to extended family. This can make it quite difficult on parents of young children; particularly those who would benefit from the respite that comes from having family nearby. It is not just having someone who will baby-sit once in a while, but the benefits are much more long term. No one ever said raising children of any age was an easy job. However, when there are grandparents or aunts and uncles close by, parents have someone they can rely on as well as go to for assistance, and most of the time, this is the emotional kind!

Sometimes Mom and Dad need a break, and there is a lot of comfort in knowing who is watching or staying with your children. Sometimes, parents just need someone to talk to who they know they can trust about things they may not want the whole neighborhood to know about. Other family members may not be able to solve all the issues, but a caring person who has a vested interest in the child, may be able to provide some guidance as well as be a good person to problem solve with. The support of extended family, especially those who are nearby, can be a gift to both parents and child. I cannot tell you how many times over the course of child-rearing I have needed someone to talk to about my children. It's not that professional help is not available. Sometimes that it is a course of action that a parent needs to pursue. But putting a plan into action is much easier when there is support for everyone concerned. Also, the child knows just how many people truly care. I think it is harder for children to show lack of respect when they have a network of people who they know believe in them.

Another plus to the "village" theory is that each person contributes in a different way to a child's development. Parents pretty much know the role they must play in raising their children. They must provide consistency, structure, love, continuity and discipline in hopes that they will raise a good person who is capable and will make a good mark on society. The "village" in your child's life can provide this same framework, but in a very different way. Grandparents, for example, have years of life experiences to share with children. And the stories they can share about the "olden days" can be quite hysterical. For instance, my mother would tell the children stories about the boat ride she took from Lebanon to the United States in 1930, when she was about 15 years old. It was so funny to listen to her tell how the rest of her family got seasick, but she didn't, so she'd play cards on deck with "the ladies!" And unbelievably, she remembered eating the most delicious tomatoes! And of course one the kids' favorite tales has to do with Fourth of July. On their first Independence Day in this country, my mom's family was so frightened by the fireworks, they thought people were shooting at them while in their home and so they called the police! And, of course, there is nothing like having an aunt, in our case a special "Gege," who did everything we couldn't do! Whether it was willingness to play a game until it was finished or buying those special treats that parents often have to say "no" to ... no one did it better than Gege. I will never forget the time that Jonathan was only a few months old and had that horrible croup. The doctor wanted to put him in the hospital but we were reluctant. He said that we could create a "tent" in his room with a humidifier and keep him in there until he was better. Gege came for three days, hardly leaving Jonathan's side and sleeping next to him at night, so Tom and I could sleep. Her devoted love for all the kids continued throughout their childhoods and is as prevalent today. The love of "the village" compares to nothing else. It is a special love and bond that is so very different than parental love.

In today's society, it is not always possible to live

near extended family, but it's amazing who can *become* family. Close friends and neighbors can be as influential in your child's life as blood relatives. Anyone who cares about you and your child will have an influence on who that child becomes. The main thing is that the people who surround you and your children and are part of your "village," need to be people who care deeply for you and your family. Nothing could be worse than having someone get too close who ends up "gossiping" to the community. But the bottom line is that we all need others, especially when we are raising our children. Everybody is different, and sometimes with another person's experiences, we can get through a difficult time or situation with a bit of grace and some peace of mind.

DINNERTIME

Dinnertime, in my humble opinion, is one of the most important parts of the day. It may not be that dinner is the most important meal, but the time you and your children spend together at this meal, is what is important. Take advantage of those years when they are little and home at dinnertime. As they grow older, their various activities will take them away from this very special and precious time. In today's society, it seems that dinner is getting later in the day, since in many families, both parents are working. Also, with the hustle and bustle of after-school activities, things get even more challenging. When your children are still very young, and possibly not even eating much besides finger foods, it is easy to let them get away with dinner in front of the television or at the table alone while you prepare the grown-up dinner or do another household job. Even at this stage, it is important to sit down with your child while they eat and to enjoy your time together for communication at whatever level it is possible. As your children become school age, the importance of dinnertime grows. Children will always have something to share, but their thoughts must appear important to those listening. Meals are very special times, and your family will come to look forward to whatever you have cooked and all sitting down together. I have heard many parents say that their children just won't talk about anything. Find things that interest your child, and begin a conversation that way. I hardly know anyone of any age who would not talk about something if they thought someone cared and would listen. I believe that people in general, and of all ages, like to share their thoughts and feelings. Being a good listener is an important lesson to learn. I also think that it is a lesson that children can learn from, and with maturity, will do for others. With some good examples in the importance of listening to others, hopefully, we will produce a generation of adults who are better listeners, for their children, spouses and co-workers.

Speaking of food (again), one of the ways our family began to look forward to dinner is because the menu was always posted on the side of the refrigerator. As a working Mom, I never had the luxury of going to the market in the middle of the day to think about what I wanted to cook that night. Instead, I found it best to plan my meals one week at a time and to post the menu. When the kids were younger and wanted to know what we were having for dinner, I would send them to the kitchen to check for themselves. As they got older, they began checking the menu on their own when they came down in the morning for breakfast. Since food was so important in our home, they would indicate their excitement for what they would be eating later that evening. In fact, it was not at all unusual for our children to make their plans based on the menu! Most of the time, they worked things out to make sure they were home in time to eat as a family. I will never forget the comment that one of Jonathans friends made when they were in high school – he told him that he was lucky to have someone who cared enough to want to cook meals that everyone wanted to be home to eat. He indicated that he never knew what he would be eating, and most of the time he was on his own for getting his dinner.

Food can bring people together – even families with teenagers!

THE FAMILY VACATION

Whenever I think of family vacations, I cannot help but think of Chevy Chase and one of his family vacation movies! Actually, ours were never quite that exciting or memorable, but the kids, as they got older added quite a bit of comedy to our trips, particularly those wonderful "car trips," where we were locked together in the "Prev" (Toyota Previa van), rocking and rolling to the music of whoever had screamed the loudest last! Dad almost always does the driving and I, as the eager to please and keep everybody happy Mom, was always in the rear, where the shock absorbers no longer were absorbing! The boys, because they tended to be more vocal, alternated the passenger's front seat, and Jennifer sat wherever she was told! Also, since she is the only one with any sense of direction besides her father, she was the navigator. The rest of us would wind up 500 miles southeast of our destination – is this the right versus left brain stuff? Truly, there is nothing that can make memories quite like those infamous family vacations. Obviously, the age of the children can make or break the situation. Given the choice, it is best to work "family" vacations around the children, their ages and interests. Our family certainly had a range of experiences in this category. How could I forget the trip to San Francisco from Los Angeles with two little boys under the age of three? At that time, it didn't seem like one restaurant in this beautiful city had a high chair! Even the restaurants in more casual settings seemed geared to a more adult clientele. How I remember the many trips to fast food restaurants near the wharf, and eating cracked crab and sourdough bread in whatever corner of the room we could find while both boys slept on the bed. And of course there was the momentous trip down Pacific Coast Highway from Monterey to San Luis Obispo. I didn't think it was possible for one little boy to throw up so many times! The scenery went completely unnoticed, as we stopped no fewer than 7 times to address this situation. But the best part of this trip was the night we spent in a tiny motel room in San Luis Obispo. It was the night/morning of Princess Diana's wedding, which I believe began airing sometime around 3 a.m. There was no way I was going to miss this once in a lifetime event, so we went to bed early, putting Jonathan in the bed furthest from the television. Andrew, in a crib, went in the closet! Well, the crib went in the closet, yes, with the sliding doors open, and Andrew went in the crib! What else to do? Anyway, it was precisely at that moment that we decided maybe car trips in constant motion were not the kind of trips we should be taking quite yet! We realized that a cabin in the mountains for a week was a more appropriate vacation that would allow us all some rest. I think it was probably about this time that someone defined the difference between a vacation and a trip – a trip is when you take the children; a vacation is when you go alone!

Nevertheless, I think "trips" with children are part of responsible parenting. They most certainly do not have to be extravagant. Especially while they are young, weekends to somewhat close locations can be as wonderful to a 5 year old as something grand. Living in southern California, we made many trips to destinations no more than 3 hours from our home, especially when all three kids were little. It was not until they were about 9, 11 and 12 that we had our first big "airplane trip," and went to the East Coast. It was fabulous and the timing was perfect. Age-wise they were ready for an extended vacation and from a school standpoint, they had begun studying some of the historical sites we were enjoying. It was prior to this trip that we came across a wonderful idea. As we were packing, one of the things causing us consternation was whether everyone should take their own camera and how much film we needed, etc. This was particularly cumbersome because at this time, the kids had Instamatic cameras (I'm dating myself), which took different film than our 35mm! Anyway, we decided to only take our good camera and we would make copies of pictures for various scrapbooks. But for the kids, we decided that beginning from the airport in San Francisco, they would collect postcards that we would attach on a ring throughout the trip. We took along a ring for each child as well as a hand-held hole punch. Every stop we made, the kids bought a postcard of their choosing, wrote a little note and dated each card, and we attached it to the ring in chronological order. These are still in their keepsake boxes as are other mementos of subsequent vacations. It turned out to be better than lots of loose pictures from cameras that weren't meant to take quality pictures. Since they each had their own scrapbooks, we made copies of special pictures for each child to have of their own.

No matter how you look at it, family vacations are generally memorable in some way. Often, it is not until years later that you can look back and say that you truly enjoyed them! While in the midst of the experience, sometimes the only thing you can think about are the temper tantrums, the finicky eater or how much more money it was costing than you thought it would! But, down the road a while, both you and the children will forget the bad things and focus on the memory. It's kind of like having a baby – if the pain didn't go away physically and emotionally, no one would have more than one child!

DON'T FORGET TO LAUGH!

I feel that humor has always been a big part of our family's dynamics. Actually, if you want to know the truth, it was often allowing myself to be laughed at that was really funny! Life is filled with many ups and downs, and they are observed from a very young age. Many things are not easily laughed at or forgotten, but light-heartedness can soften even an unhappy situation. In my many years of working with children, I have found myself being silly or making the children laugh during a session. Sometimes I would get the strangest looks, and when I ask them "don't you laugh at home," many would tell me that they don't! I can't even imagine raising children without laughing! Being silly is okay. Allow your children to know that you are capable of acting like a child and that certain things can be acceptable to laugh at. I would sing silly, homemade songs to tunes we were all familiar with to the kids when they were growing up. They laughed at me, I laughed at myself and we shared a special moment! It really doesn't take much to make children laugh. What it does take is some vulnerability on the parent's part. When kids grow up this way, they often develop a sense of humor early on and will often enjoy adults at a younger age. Even teachers at the early grades will say things in the classroom that they know will often go above the heads of many of the children. But there are always a few kids who "get it!" These children have been introduced to humor through their surroundings. Not only in things that we knowingly observe as funny, but in a somewhat deeper way, that is actually a bit more sophisticated, requiring a little more maturity.

SPEECH & LANGUAGE

"Language" is probably the simplest concept that exists, and yet one of the most difficult to explain. As a speech and language pathologist, I must explain this difference many, many times. "Speech," professionally speaking, refers to a child's articulation - how they pronounce their words/sounds. When someone says they cannot understand your child, they are most likely referring to his/her articulation. Speech is developmental, and comes in stages based on a child's age and motor development. There are many norms that parents can access in various child development books available or on the internet. Generally speaking, however, sounds develop somewhat in the following order:

3 year level – B, P, M, W, H
4 year level – T, D, N, K, G, NG, Y
5 year level – F
6 year level – V, L, SH, ZH, CH, J
7 year level – R, S, Z, TH

No two children are the same, and many children will develop all these sounds easily and early in their development, while other children seem to be more "text-book!" Babbling at 5-7 months is followed by jargon (strings of sounds or syllables produced with a variety of stress and intonation) from 8-24 months. By 12 months, the child is starting to put together the sounds to form "true" words. Speech development requires maturation of many muscles that evolve over a 4-5 year period of time. Others, of course, will benefit from speech therapy to help them learn how to produce the sounds and then use them appropriately. It is not at all uncommon to have many children in a kindergarten class having difficulty with /l/, /r/, /s/ and /th/. Developmentally, these sounds do not develop until later. But it is always good to have your child listened to by a speech therapist if you are at all concerned. Early intervention is always the best route.

Typically, a child at 18-24 months is 25-50% intelligible to the unfamiliar listener. They should be 50-75% intelligible at 2-3 years and 80% intelligible at 3-4 years. At 4-5 years of age, the child should be 90-100% intelligible, although there still may be some articulation errors for later developing sounds. Remember .... Many 5-6 year olds will have difficulty with /l/, /r/,/s/ and /th/! All three of our kids needed a little speech "help!"

"Language" is better defined in terms of understanding and expression. How your child follows directions, uses appropriate vocabulary, uses social skills and interprets context cues are all under the "language" umbrella. Language is happening all around us and we need language to read, write, do math and science and follow directions. Language begins the moment your child is born. When you talk, sing and read to your child, you are introducing language. It is in poetry when they hear the rhyming words and in music through the lyrics of a song. When you read and ask your child to point to the "cow", you are teaching receptive language skills. When you point and ask your child what that animal is called, expressive language is taking place. Having your child follow simple directions such as getting you something from the other room or asking them to get on their pajamas and brush their teeth, is teaching the child to listen and follow sequential steps. Talk, talk, and talk to your child so that they hear speech and language all the time. But talking to a child without giving them an opportunity to respond or not listening to what they have to say is not what this is about. I hear many parents say that they read to their children, but there is no interaction going on. When you read a book, regardless of the level, give children the opportunity to "communicate." If it is a picture book, talk about the pictures on the page or what is happening in the scene. Introduce vocabulary and answer the child's questions, even though sometimes you are tired and want to quit. If your child is one of those that will ask questions forever, introduce the concept of "just one" question and then move on. They will learn what this means. When reading "chapter" books or those with more verbiage, stop from time to time to see if your child is comprehending what is being read. Words are great but if the understanding is not there, the words will not turn into a story and remain just words. Teach your child to "read" the visual cues in the pictures. Why is the girl on the page pouting when all the other children are painting? Why is the fish in the fishbowl fretting as the cat sitting next to it is peering in? Some children will learn these skills on their own, while others need someone to help them to "see." As you probe and ask questions, you will be amazed by the things your child is learning from his environment.

Sentence Length

Sentence length is looked at in terms of months of age and meaningfulness of language.

Up to two years of age, single words are expected. They are usually a noun (mama, dada, cup, car), verbs (eat, sleep, go) and attributes (more, big, blue).

At **22-24 months**, two-term phrases are appropriate. This would include phrases such as "mommy go", "more juice", "in cup", "my car", "no sleep" and "dog eat." These phrases, although short, communicate effectively what the child wants/needs/sees.

At **24-30 months**, three-term phrases emerge. Included might be "daddy go car", "sleep blankie here", "car not go" and "walk my school".

At **30-36 months**, four-five word sentences are becoming the norm. "I sleep big bed", "daddy go to work" and "I like cars not trains" are examples.

Pragmatic Language Development

Pragmatic language is the language we use in social situations. Pragmatic language is used in three main ways:

1. Language used for greetings, informing, demanding, requesting or promising.
2. Changing/adapting language to meet the needs/expectations of a listener or situation.
3. Following conversational rules such as for turn-taking, staying on topic and rephrasing when misunderstood. There are also nonverbal behaviors in communication such as eye contact, facial expressions and distance between the speaker and the listener.

The most important thing here is that if you have a concern, it is never too early to check it out. Your pediatrician is usually the first person you would talk to, since they screen speech and language during well baby exams. Before the age of three, Regional Center in your area will also assess and provide services if needed. Once a child is three years old, your local school district becomes the responsible party for assessing and determining eligibility. Beyond that, there are a bevy of speech pathologists in private practice to assist if there is a need.

"I DON'T LOVE YOU MORE – I LOVE YOU DIFFERENT!"

The idea for this chapter literally "popped" into my head one morning. A very hard worker, Jennifer was in the second day of finals in the Fall semester of her junior year of high school. Although she had been doing quite well in her six honors classes, she found herself teetering between grades in two classes. I could see the stress in her eyes knowing that some of these finals could determine which way her grade in that class went. I personally get a lot of peace from prayer, but generally I think of myself as a "private prayer" and don't like to impose it on anyone, even family. As I was wanting to pray for Jennifer, and I hoped she was praying for herself, I thought that it would be good for both of us to pray together that her exams would go well. I think Jennifer thought I was crazy when I proposed my idea, but being who she is, agreed to follow in suit. We held hands and said a simple prayer, tears rolling down both our cheeks, and then we shared a very special hug. I felt her arms tightly around my neck and knew that what we had shared was special. I looked at her and the words just came out – "I don't love you more or less – I love you different." I knew immediately that this had to be a chapter in my book. For as long as I can remember, I have heard people say that "I'm Mom's favorite," or "Dad loves you more." I don't think this has anything to do with love. It has everything to do with our own personal relationships with each other. Just because a child is born of two people, it does not mean that we are all alike and totally compatible. Each child is born with their very own personality which comes from a combination of their parents as well as a little bit of their own. The dispute over "nurture" versus "nature" continues, I'm sure, but this does not enter into the fact that each of us is who we are, and we relate to each person in our lives differently. People are always saying that girls are easier or boys are easier, but again I have to say that I believe it's the combination of personalities that help us to deal with people, even our children. Look at twins – born at almost the same precise moment and having spent many months in utero together, parents will tell you that they each have their own personality. How can we expect to get along with each of our children in exactly the same way? It's impossible! This is where the "I don't love you more or less, just different" theory comes into play. As I consider my own children, all born fairly close together, I see that I have such a different , yet wonderful relationship with each one. Jonathan, the "talker" and "listener," is an observant person who has no difficulty communicating. Lucky is my beautiful daughter-in-law, Meredith, who married Jonathan! When most of the world's wives are complaining that their husbands don't know how to communicate, there will be Jonathan, listening attentively and "talking" about his feelings! Wow, what a concept for a man! We used to walk and talk together when he was younger and we were living in Irvine. Our special bond continued with our 2+ hours of conversations over coffee that started at the local Starbuck's in Danville during his high school years. What a treat for me to have such a break, and to be so lucky to know my son that well. Today I am blessed to hear his voice most everyday. He often calls me in the morning on his way to work and we share stories of what we cooked for dinner the previous night or what vegetable is in-season this month at the farmer's market! He has always been a safe person for me to talk to and I always value his thoughts and love. I know I will always look at Jonathan with pride and look forward to him being my "friend" forever.

Andrew is all heart. When he was little, I would look into his eyes and I felt that I could see his soul. It took a different perspective on "mothering" for me to really know who Andrew was. He had his own opinions from a very young age. It was with Andrew that I learned the term "pick your battles." He has probably taught me the most about people, because I had to learn about him. Andrew was the person in our house that seemed different from the rest of us. While most of us were willing to just "play the game" in whatever situation we were in, Andrew was always questioning and wanting to know "why!" As he got older, he also learned to pick his battles, and maturity taught him how to guide himself through life's various situations. He has turned into a wonderful, mature, and responsible young man. Every single time I worry about him, he proves to me that he has his life together and is working towards his goals. Although a different kind of communicator than his brother, Andrew is equally as loving and concerned and safe for me to talk to. He always makes sure that I know his comings and goings, especially with all the traveling he does for work. He reminds me that he is only a phone call away, no matter where he is. Andrew was always a "cuddler" as a child and would be quick to plop himself in my lap or near me to watch T.V. or read a book. When he was in high school, we had our best chats late at night when everyone else was in bed. Andrew was always the night owl, and I learned to use that time to have our heart-to-heart talks. These days, we will often have breakfast on a weekend morning, talking about everything from USC football to vacations to work. He, too, values what I think and I know that Andrew will always have me in his heart. I know I will always look at Andrew with pride and look forward to him being my "friend" forever.

Jennifer and I have what I think of as the "mother-daughter" relationship. We are very similar in our likes and dislikes and sometimes I wonder if I've turned her into a mirror image of myself, or if this is truly who she is! We've been very lucky in that we have not had many of those mother-daughter incidents that people often talk about. We laugh together and have enjoyed the many renditions of songs from "Grease" that we would blare out in the car while driving the streets of Danville! What a sight that must have been to the onlookers! She is so easy for me to talk to, but I have to be careful as she is extremely sensitive. I watch her and am amazed at this new generation of strong young women so different than I was at her age. She has learned much earlier than I did how to take care of herself, especially emotionally. I think this is a responsibility my generation of Moms needed to do for their children, especially their daughters. Women today are stronger and better prepared to take care of themselves. They truly can be anything and anyone they want to be, and I see in Jennifer the inner strength that has allowed her to know that herself. I know I will always look at Jennifer with pride and I look forward to her being my "friend" forever.

FAMILY MEETINGS

In our home, I'm the CIC (Chick in Charge)! This is a designation that my husband gave me many years ago and it kind of stuck! When the children were still at home, I was huge on family meetings. I'm not sure why, but sometimes I think it was just to hear myself talk! Truthfully, I am a planner from the get go, and I have always believed in letting everyone know what the plan was as well as to get their input when decisions needed to be made. Family meetings at the younger stages of life were usually accompanied by dessert! There we go again... food has always been such an incentive at our house! I would make something that I knew everyone would eat and then begin the meeting. As the kids got into the mid-grade school years, I would often put together an agenda! I know it might sound silly, but that way I could talk while they had something in front of them to read. It kept them more engaged! You're probably asking yourself, "What does this crazy lady have to talk so much about?" Well, first of all, family meetings were usually every couple of months, unless there were things I really felt we needed to talk about in between. And most family meetings were FUN! For instance, if we were going on a trip during the summer, I would gather the troops to talk about what each of them waned to see or do. When taking a vacation, it seems that everyone, even a five-year-old, has something they don't want to miss. I am a great planner, but sometimes I miss the boat! I remember the year we went to San Francisco when the kids were all under eight years of age. Jonathan wanted to go see the U.S.S. Pompanito, a navy submarine. Andrew wanted to go to Alcatraz and Jennifer wanted a sundae from the Ghirardelli Chocolate Factory! Now, there's a good chance that we might have had all these experiences, but the fact that they were able to contribute their ideas and for sure get to do something they wanted, made it all that more enjoyable.

Some of my favorite meetings were the ones I called for no good reason. I'm pretty mushy and totally in love with my kids. I would sometimes call a meeting so I could tell them how much I loved them and how proud Dad and I were of them. We lavished our children with praise from a very early age. There was no one we could ever love more than them. I would often get them one of those sappy cards that tell kids how incredible they are, of course, choosing just the right one for each child. Then there would be a "little treat" inside. It was never anything great or expensive. Usually it would be a gift certificate for ice cream or a few dollars to do with what they wanted .... just a reminder of how much they were loved.

PETS

This will be a short chapter. *I DON'T DO PETS!* Now, I am sure there are a zillion of you out there that are thinking how awful this must be. I, on the other hand feel that at least I am honest about my feelings. As a full time working mom with three young children and a husband who commuted about 2 hours each way to work or was often traveling, I just did not see how I could take care of one more thing! We did, though, have our fair share of goldfish and box turtles, but these are truly low maintenance pets! I would urge families to do what is best for them. No matter what a child says, they are not going to be the one taking care of the animals. Generally, it is going to become the responsibility of MOM, and if you don't want that job, find alternatives that work for you. We used to say that someday the kids would be sitting in a psychologist's office saying, "Everything that's wrong with us today is all Mom's fault – she didn't let us have a dog!" What a coincidence that Jonathan would be a psychiatrist!!! Needless to say, all the kids love pets and I know that they will be a part of their households. And as "grandparents," we get to visit, love and spoil them!

WORKING VS STAY-AT-HOME MOMS

The decision to stay at home with your children or to work is never an easy one for families. So many factors play a role in the choices that need to be made. Economics is probably the single most influential factor in making the decision to work or not. For many families in today's society, two working parents is a way of life. To meet the ever rising cost of living, save for the future and meet the needs of today, many moms must work to help ends meet. Some women are lucky enough to be able to work part-time, allowing them the "best of both worlds." They have time at home with their children, while still being able to dabble in the workplace and enjoy the interaction with other adults. They contribute to the household budget and get a bit of a respite from child rearing, as well. This is truly one place where it is "quality not quantity" that makes the difference. I speak from experience here. I have worked all but one of the years we have had children. For many of those years, I was full time. When Jennifer was about 6 years old, I began working part time. It was amazing how creative I could get with my schedule! Some years, I worked three full days, while other years, I would work each day 9:00 to 2:00, so I did not need to use daycare much anymore. There were many years where I felt my entire paycheck was going to the baby-sitter! But it didn't, and what I did make was important and contributed to the family budget. Also, I had worked hard to get my Master's degree, and wanted to keep myself active in a profession that I loved. And if you are fortunate enough to be able to stay home, please enjoy this wonderful opportunity you have been given. Staying home all day to raise children is truly a thankless job and only in the many years to come, will you reap the benefits of all the time you have put into your kids. Only if you have done it do you know how hard it really is! Being at your child's beckon call all day is not easy! The responsibility you feel to make sure your child is healthy and happy and benefitting from you being there for them is huge. Either way, whatever you have to do or choose to do, remember that both kinds of parenting has its challenges and perks, and each day you might feel differently as to what kind of day it feels like! Just keep tucked in the back of your mind that your kids are a gift and that this is the time to "make memories."

THE POWER HUG

This is probably the most ridiculous tradition in this book! Imagine a grown woman standing three feet away from her already taller than her child, moving forward to embrace the child, hugging with a "wiggle" and then planting three kisses on each cheek, accompanied by a puckering sound!! Do not ask me how this started, but some time ago, during the middle school/high school years, when the kids were apprehensive about a particular test, we began the "Power Hug." The intent was that they would take my strength and confidence with them as they went into the test. Of course, we know that this cannot make the difference, particularly for a child who did not study, but after a few good test scores, none of the kids would leave home without the "hug!" I suppose this would go in the same category as rabbit's feet and lucky pennies, but either way, it is a tradition that continued throughout high school, with occasional "hugs" over the phone for college finals! Whether it's been a test or an interview, there is something to be said for the "Power

Hug." We were all disappointed when it didn't work, but we continued to persevere. Many times, the "hug" worked in reverse, with me being the recipient. If I had a difficult meeting to attend or an extremely busy day, the kids were there for me, although I might add that because of their strength, I often asked for a "gentle" version! Again, it's about creating a bond. I hope all my children will share the "power hug" with their kids someday.

GIFTEDNESS COMES IN MANY FLAVORS

Educationally speaking, gifted children score a "magic number" on a standardized intelligence test that qualifies them to participate in certain extra-curricular activities, special classes or various programs provided in or outside of the classroom setting, depending on the school district. But these children only make up a minute number of our population who test at this "magic number" or above. Yes, it is a good indicator of a child's potential, but what a child does with his potential is what really makes the difference. How many children do we all know who are very smart but not making it in the school setting? Parents often express concern that teachers are not motivating enough, or the content of the material not stimulating. Maybe this very bright child would rather write stories or draw pictures than do the typical school curriculum. And what about the child who is "average?" They do okay in school, getting some A's and mostly B's, but this child can play soccer like no one else around. Or what about the child who has Down Syndrome, but is a gifted artist who sells his paintings for lots of money! Then, of course, there is the child who is not the greatest student, does not have any special sports talent and can't paint or draw. But this child has developed into one of the kindest, most caring people, who is always willing to help others and is a terrific friend. Would he not be considered gifted in his own right? "Giftedness" truly does come in lots of flavors.

"YES" AND "NO"

Finding the happy medium between when to say yes and when to say no is the probably the hardest thing to do as a parent. In my work, I have observed that many parents fear saying "no" because they are afraid that their children will not love them. Nothing could be further from the truth. All children want and need parameters in their lives – they just don't know it! The sooner you begin enforcing certain rules, the happier both you and your child will be. Using the "no" word when children are toddlers and preschoolers is particularly hard because the heartfelt tears and sweet smiles can easily turn a parent's heart. BUT – those little darlings grow up! Now they are bigger than you and those sweet faces aren't nearly as cute! My sister and I were always brought up knowing that there were certain situations and places that weren't meant for kids. With my family, the kids had "child-proof" rooms, such as the family room. However, the formal living room and dining rooms were off-limits. I happen to love "pretty things" and the living room coffee tables were adoringly set with treasures we had collected throughout our marriage. This was not a room for pudgy little hands, with sticky, clumsy finger! Now in no way is this meant to be derogatory, because anyone who knows me knows that I adored my "little darlings", but I also loved my home. And part of my happiness came from the fact that I could look at one part of my house and knew that it was a place to entertain adults and enjoy some special things in my life. If this does not pertain to you, then by no means should you feel obligated to do such with your home. However, then you also can't yell at your child when they break something that you consider priceless. Unless they know their limits, it's a free for all! Plus, I do believe, as I said before, that children need limits. What better place to teach this skill but in your own home.

Also, remember, that as a child gets older, so do the stakes. When you are saying "no" to a younger child it is often associated with wanting something to eat right before a meal, or wanting a toy when you are out shopping. Each year that they get older, so do the "toys." When my children were little, toys were still the kind of toys we think of from a generation ago. Today's toys include computer and video games. At upwards of $40 - $50 for some of these things, once you begin overindulging your child, the harder it will be when you really want to say "no." My life experiences have taught me that life is totally unpredictable. One day everything is going along like a dream and the next day can take a 180 degree turn. Making children aware of the costs of things early on, and teaching them the importance of saving, will be one of the best gifts you can give your child.

The "N" word does not apply to only tangible objects. Actually, more importantly is knowing **when** to say "no" so that you can use if most effectively! This sort of moves into the "pick your battles" theory, which I was introduced to when our children were still very young. I think that with children, and some more than others, we feel that all we do is fight. This gets old very quickly, and can be quite exhausting emotionally; particularly on parents (kids seem to have better stamina for this)! Also, it makes it difficult to bond with your child, because you are always battling. As is the same with tangible objects and gifts, the stakes go up as children get older. When little, their independence and desires are still within your control and observation. As they get older, they want things such as more allowance, extended curfews and taking the car out of the parameters of what feels comfortable for you. This is when it is good to really think about what you say "yes" and "no" to. Save the big guns for the biggest battles, and realize that it is permission to do the little things that will actually give you ammunition later when you need it. Parents who always say "no" find it more difficult to justify their position. If you have worked with and listened to your child, you have entrusted them with a certain amount of responsibility and now they are more likely to respect your reasons and concerns when they want to do something you really don't want them to do. Of course, there will always be those times when you battle it out irregardless of what each of you says, but I have found that when there is a healthy respect between parents and children, fewer battles ensue.

THE HIGH MAINTENANCE CHILD

Most everyone knows someone who has a "high maintenance child." By this term, I don't mean the child who out of necessity is needy. Due to physical reasons and developmental delays, some children require a lot of attention. Here, I am referring to the typical-developing child who makes parenting a full-time job! I like this term much better than speaking of "difficult" children or any of those other terms we use. The high maintenance child does not mean this child is bad or constantly misbehaving. It means that he/she keeps you on your toes most of the time! Often, these children are very bright, and I think sometimes too smart for their own good! They are quick thinkers and often have retorts for everything that is said to them. I know a lot of parents who will say that their child is "perfect" at school, but at home, will give parents a run for their money! This child sounds very smart to me! The key to raising this type of child is **consistency** and staying one step in front of him! When children know the routine and expectations, it is harder for diversions, especially at the younger ages. This is where it is really important to "pick your battles." Does it really matter if they go to school and their pants and shirts don't match? And if they don't have breakfast, will they starve before the first recess and snack? Most children are resilient from quite a young age. Adults are the ones who grow tired faster!

PLEASE AND THANK YOU

After my 30+ years of working with children and raising my own, I truly believe in the please and thank you concept. I have found that when you are respectful to children, they learn to be respectful back to you. Children are people, too, and the fact that they are younger than oneself, does not mean that they should not be treated with and taught respect. Over the years, I have realized that even when working with special needs children, those that are capable to "thanking you" will do so if they have models to follow. Learning to respect someone comes from being respected. I am not saying here that children should be undisciplined. On the contrary, children need rules and structure, but even these can be delivered with respect. When children see and hear the adults in their lives using their best manners, they too, will follow in suit. Now you may have to subtly remind them for some years, but eventually they will surprise you one day by spontaneously using all the skills you have been teaching them. Respect is the key to relationships, every single one!

"SITTOISMS" – SITTO'S WORDS OF WISDOM

Sitto is my mom. This is the Arabic word for Grandma and our Sitto was the quintessential Sitto. If you could imagine that "old country" type of grandmother who adored her family and did everything possible for them, that would be my mom. Sitto, as we all called her, has passed away and is so desperately missed. At the ripe old age of 90, she still had her dry whit and sense of humor and her adoration for her family. After Sitto's death, our family found that hardly a day could go by when we weren't quoting her endlessly or remembering some of her wise words of wisdom! Sitto taught all that met her about the unconditional love of family. Not a day went by that I did not talk with her, and probably what I miss the most about her being gone is hearing her tell me she loved me every single day of my life. In fact, whenever anyone in our immediate family speaks to one another, we almost always end the conversation with "I love you." Who will ever love us like we love each other? And why not tell someone you love them when you do!

Sitto had such a way with words! One of my favorites of her sayings was, "Didn't they look in the mirror before they left the house?!" Sitto always believed in looking, acting and dressing appropriately. She would utter words in Arabic that, translated, meant, "Shame on you," whenever she saw someone who should not have left their house looking they way they did! We would laugh hysterically at what she noticed, and in most instances, she was right.

Sitto also had some phrases that only sound beautiful when she said them in Arabic, but translated, the meaning is still poignant. For instance, she would always remind me that I could never know the depth of her love for me and my sister until we had children of our own. Boy... was she right! She would remind us that "the world is a Mother," meaning that for most, when things are good or bad, we always tend to want to connect with our mothers. They provide that unconditional love that no one else can and as a society we tend to want to share our joys and our sorrows with them.

Another one of Sitto's famous sayings was ".... if God is willing." I went to see her most days when she was in a skilled nursing facility. And everyday, I would say, "I'll see you tomorrow Mom." And each time she would respond in Arabic, "If God is willing." She would bless me, kiss me and tell me how much she loved me. It's hard to get much better than this. This is what I miss every single day of my life ....

I feel sad that my wonderful daughter-in-law and son-in-law were not able to meet Sitto. But I am convinced we have made her memory very alive for them. All of the children, including my nephew Nicholas, have written college essays about Sitto. We should all be so lucky that 17 and 18 year olds think we are so special that they want to share stories about us! Sitto didn't have anything but her love to share with her family. Even though she was not a young grandmother, she managed to sit on the floor and play with all the kids. She had a small blue bucket of pennies and at a very young age, taught the children how to play Blackjack and Poker with those pennies! She was hysterical! Sitto had just the right mix of teaching the kids that they could win or someone else could win, and it was okay. She loved feeding them Arabic food and they would eat anything she put in front of them! She would often have them sit on the floor, give them a kitchen towel to put over their laps, and then feed them! And they would do whatever she said! She was a tough cookie and didn't believe in disrespectful children! And boy... did they listen to her! Over the years, the love just grew and grew.

Especially poignant was the time that my mom had a heart attack. The children were approximately 6, 5 and 3. I got the call from my sister who said that the doctors wanted to take Sitto into surgery but she refused to go until she saw her grandchildren! I could never forget that drive from Irvine to the San Fernando Valley at 3:00 in the afternoon on a workday! We got there, though, and everyone saw Sitto before she had her operation. Jennifer happened to have her My Little Pony, Apple Jack, with her. She gave it to Sitto to have during the surgery (somehow I don't think it made its way to the operating room)! Either way, that became a bond for the two of them and Apple Jack is still with Sitto today.

When we lived in the Bay area, and the kids were about ten years and a bit, it was not uncommon for my sister, (Gege to the kids) and my mom, to drive to Harris Ranch, halfway between San Francisco and Los Angeles, to meet and take one or two of the kids for special time with them. A week or two later, we would either meet half way again or one of us would drive the kids all the way home. This continued through high school and beyond. Each of the children spent time with Sitto and Gege during college too, living there when they did not want or could not come home for vacations. I still remember the thrill in my mom's voice when she knew they were coming and would cook ANYTHING their hearts desired, and Arabic food is not that easy to prepare! Our lives have been blessed by Sitto and Gege. Today, as I find out that I am going to be a Sitto to a beautiful baby girl, I pray that someday I will be the quintessential Sitto, too.

SAY "I LOVE YOU"

After my Dad passed away, I realized the importance of telling people I love that I loved them. Thankfully, I told my dad I loved him the last time I saw him alive. This was particularly poignant because I never had the opportunity again and I realized how much it meant to me that he knew how I felt. I feel that we give and get a lot of emotional strength from others when we say "I love you." In our family, it is not uncommon to utter these words. But "I love you" should not be restricted to family use! I have come to a time in my life, that if I love you, I'm going to tell you! And you don't have to say it back! There are many people with whom I am acquainted that do not feel it is appropriate to use these words outside their immediate family. Be true to how you feel. Others that I know will not initiate "I love you" or "love you" but I know they do. Don't get me wrong – I don't take this lightly and say it in an off the cuff manner. What works for me is to validate and show appreciation for those who do something that helps improve the quality of my life.

There are times in your life when you come across someone who is not your family and with whom you "click!" And you genuinely begin to care about this person and realize that time spent with them makes you happier and feel better. These are the people I love.

It's terrible to be confronted with a time in your life when you have to say "good-bye" and you wish you had told the person more often how much you care and appreciate them. These are the words of the "older generation," and I am fortunate to have been brought up with so much love in my life. I had parents who adored my sister and I, and would do ANYTHING they could to make life better for us. Fortunately, we were able to do the same things for our children. Some might say that is called "spoiled," but I think they are loved so deeply, that all they know how to do is give love back, which they do over and over again every day. When I hear stories about people who do not keep in touch with their families, especially elderly parents, I find it incredibly sad. When I lost my mom and realized I had no more parents, I felt like an orphan. It was such a vulnerable feeling – at least for me.

WHAT DO YOU MEAN MY SON DIDN'T GET INTO STANFORD?

The Spring of 1997 was a wonderful time. Jonathan was about to graduate from high school and he had applied to numerous schools within California. Day after day, the mailbox would contain a "thick" envelope with acceptance letters and information about the school. Jonathan was also blessed to have been given scholarships at many of the schools he applied to, which was wonderful as well. Then, on an auspicious April afternoon, a "thin" envelope arrived! What! It couldn't be a rejection - it had to be a simple acceptance with information to follow! And from Stanford!!! As Jonathan opened the letter and began reading, we quickly realized that this was not a "happy" note! What do you mean you don't want my son at your school?! I was sure it had to be a mistake! He had been accepted EVERYWHERE and they were all so happy to have my precious first-born attend their school! Well, this would not do! I immediately picked up the phone and dialed the number at the bottom of the letter. I had no qualms asking to speak directly with the director of admissions (those were the days that someone actually answered the phone)! Surprisingly, it was quite easy! I politely explained to him that I thought he had made a mistake and sent Jonathan the wrong envelope. The gentleman graciously asked me to hold on while he pulled Jonathan's file. A few minutes later, he was back on the phone. "Oh, Mrs. Still, I see here you have a very bright son," he said. I confirmed that I was aware of my child's abilities. "Oh, and such a good grade point average and so many accolades," he said again. As he rummaged through the file, he reiterated several times all the good things he saw. Then came the questions!!! "Mrs. Still, I see your son has taken quite a few years of Spanish. He must be quite proficient. Did Jonathan travel to a foreign country to help others learn English or to work with the disadvantaged?" "Well, no", I replied. "Oh .... I see that your son plays the piano and has written some songs. That's wonderful, Mrs. Still! Has he ever played at Carnegie Hall?" Oh my gosh ... I could see where this was going. "And ... does he play any sports that would allow him to compete on a school team here at Stanford?" Wow!!! Again the answer was "no." The admissions officer gently informed me that Jonathan had not been accepted but that he was indeed, a wonderful candidate. Talk about a humbling experience! I still don't regret that phone call and it truly has made for many a funny story!

I guess where I'm going with this is that as a parent, particularly a mother, there isn't anything you won't do for your children. And, if ever you think they have been wronged, it's amazing how the hairs on the back of your neck stand up and you find yourself defending them as fiercely as a wild animal!!! Oh well, Jonathan went off to Claremont McKenna, a small private college, and did beautifully. It truly was everything he had wanted in a college experience and perfect for him. Things do happen for a reason....

LETTING GO

This is a concept that no one can prepare you for. A parent knows all along that their children are a gift for about 18 years, at least that is the approximate amount of time we can expect them to live at home under our rules! But the day that you are supposed to "let them fly" or "cut the apron strings," is probably the most difficult day ever. That day is different for every child, because some do this sooner and others later. Some children start the "letting go" process themselves, but this is about the parents letting go... especially Mom! This is often the day you have all been waiting for. Afterall, if they're off to college, they have worked hard through school, developing good study habits, getting good SAT scores and good grades. All of these things were done in preparation for this wonderful time of knowing that your child would be moving on with their life. And if they're living at home while pursuing their education or working, life will never be the same. They're 18 years old, the magical age that someone determined that kids no longer need their parents for anything that they don't want us to be involved in! Then why does it feel so bad? Why does it hurt so much when you walk to the end of the hall and their bedroom is clean and spotless, and the bathroom doesn't have toothpaste and hair all over the sink? Why does it hurt so much when they come home for several weeks at Christmas and you can't stop crying when they leave? True, the house is clean again, there's tons less wash, the food bill is once again manageable and you don't have to stay up waiting for anyone. But there is also no buzz at the kitchen table during dinner, no 2 hour coffee breaks "just because" and a lot fewer "I love you, Mom." Even today and at their age, I love so much when they are home and miss them so much when they leave. “Letting go” truly was a bittersweet experience, which I realized I had no control over. I watched many of my friends handle this situation, and I must say that most everyone felt somewhat the same. Even the parents of the high maintenance children admitted that they missed their kids. I can’t forget the time that Jennifer, the last of our three, left for college. Now mind you, we were living in Orange County then and she was only 30 or so miles away at USC! I was devastated! I hardly could function. Finally, I mustered all my energy and got dressed to go to the Build-A-Bear store! I HAD to send Jennifer something so she would know how much I missed her, so I made her a USC cheerleader bear! Yes ... I cried hysterically at each station, stuffing this precious bear, putting a voice message in her paw (our favorite saying, “Is it time to play yet?”) and making her a birth certificate. I would remind each parent of a young child that these precious days would pass quickly and that someday they would feel just the same way! I can’t imagine what the patrons thought that day – they are probably still talking about that crazy lady who upset their little children crying through the store! No matter that I cried 6 hours up Highway 5 from Los Angeles to Danville when we dropped Jonathan off at Claremont-McKenna and Andrew at USC! Unlike Jennifer, who I left in her room crying, the boys were so ready for me to get in the car and go home! Nevertheless, it didn't comfort me that they were okay... because I wasn't!!!

Either way, the greatest comfort comes from seeing your child truly happy. Nothing feels better than knowing they are being successful and happy in their new home, whether it's a college dorm, an apartment or truly their very own house. When they call from school to share the latest events, it touches a soft spot in your heart that lets you know that this is the way it was always intended to be. Although the longing is there to still be the "mommy" or "daddy" of years gone by, life lets us know that the time to "let go" has come. But trust me – they're never gone forever! It's amazing how quickly they call when they don't feel well, need money or just need the comforts of home for a little while. And this is the way it's meant to be, too! They should know that home is there for them. Even though they do have other "homes," no matter how old they get, no one is too old for a warm hug or some comfort food that only Mom or Dad knows how to make.

ADULT CHILDREN

I never thought I would enjoy any stage of my children's development except for the one we were in! Little did I know that each stage brought its own personality for each of the kids, and that having "friends" who are your kids is GREAT!! There is nothing more rewarding than looking at your adult child and muttering to yourself, "I like this person!" We have had so much fun since all the kids have gone to college. Of course, there were times when I thought they would never "grow up," but with each passing college year emerged a more responsible, caring young person who was great to be with. What amazed me the most was that they enjoyed having us around and would bring their friends home for good food and just to hang out. We have always been included in football games and tailgating festivities and are the "token parents"! We are delighted and honored.

There's such a new honesty that has developed along with this transformation. Sometimes I don't like it because they can be brutally honest and at times I don't want to hear what they have to say. Afterall, now they are adults asserting their views on life! However, it doesn't take long to realize that once your children are more independent, they are not going to ask your permission for many things any more. But when they want your opinion because they truly value what you think, that is the most incredible feeling. I treasure the words they write to me in their cards for birthdays and holidays and carry those cards with me all of the time. They are a constant reminder of how blessed I am.

THE MOUNTAIN GOES TO MOHAMMAD

With children married and all in bustling careers, I have adopted the "mountain goes to Mohammed" philosophy! Not to say that my husband and I aren't still busy with our jobs, but there is no doubt in my mind that we miss them more than they miss us! This is not a bad thing, but it's funny how once you are a parent, no matter the age of the children, they still are your kids. I like to believe that any opportunity we have to see them is yet another gift in our lives. As we grow older and they become more involved in their own families, I believe this attitude will behoove us even more. It's much harder to gather up the "troops" and get them all in the car than it is for two grown-ups to drive a bit to see the loves of their lives. Hopefully, good health will provide us with many years of being able to visit our kids and to-be grandchildren. After all, this is all part of the "village."

ASK YOUR KIDS

I once asked my children what they thought was the key to making them who they are today. Collectively, they agreed that they felt they could talk to us about anything and that we would listen and give honest input. They also felt that trusting them and not having a formal curfew was a huge incentive to continuing this type of relationship. It's true! Our kids never had a curfew, and yet, they were always home at a time that we mutually agreed upon. In those few instances that they were running a little late, they would always call - and that was before the days of cell phones!!! The bottom line is if you respect your kids they will respect you back. But it has to start early. There are many ways of showing respect to your child prior to their teenage years. This will make it easier when you NEED them to respect your decisions. We also believed in the "tell me the truth, even if it hurts" policy! I can't stand it when someone lies. I have always told the kids that I would rather hear the truth and not agree with their choice, than be lied to. I am sure there have been some lies during those years, but I think they were minimized due to our openness with each other. This really pertains to when they get older and are not asking you for permission any longer. For instance, when the kids were in college and going somewhere or with someone they thought I might not approve of (as though I had a choice), I would always ask them to tell me where they were going and a phone number. Sometimes at the beginning they would fight me on this, but now I get whole itineraries! I have never once picked up the phone to call them, but they call me! I don't think it's out of fear or guilt, but rather about sharing enjoyment. I think they genuinely know I love them and care.

EPILOGUE

Today I am happy. Jonathan wrote to me from Paris about all the wonderful food he was eating and said "I love you Mom" .... Andrew called me while on a weekend get-a-way to say, "I love you Mom" .... And Jennifer called with a crack in her voice because she didn't feel well and was tired ... and said "I love you Mom." I am a lucky and truly blessed Mom.

www.ingramcontent.com/pod-product-compliance
Ingram Content Group UK Ltd.
Pitfield, Milton Keynes, MK11 3LW, UK
UKHW040557210726
13854UKWH00007B/1358

9 781105 709197